Sofia Travel Highlights

Best Attractions & Experiences

Todd MacIntyre

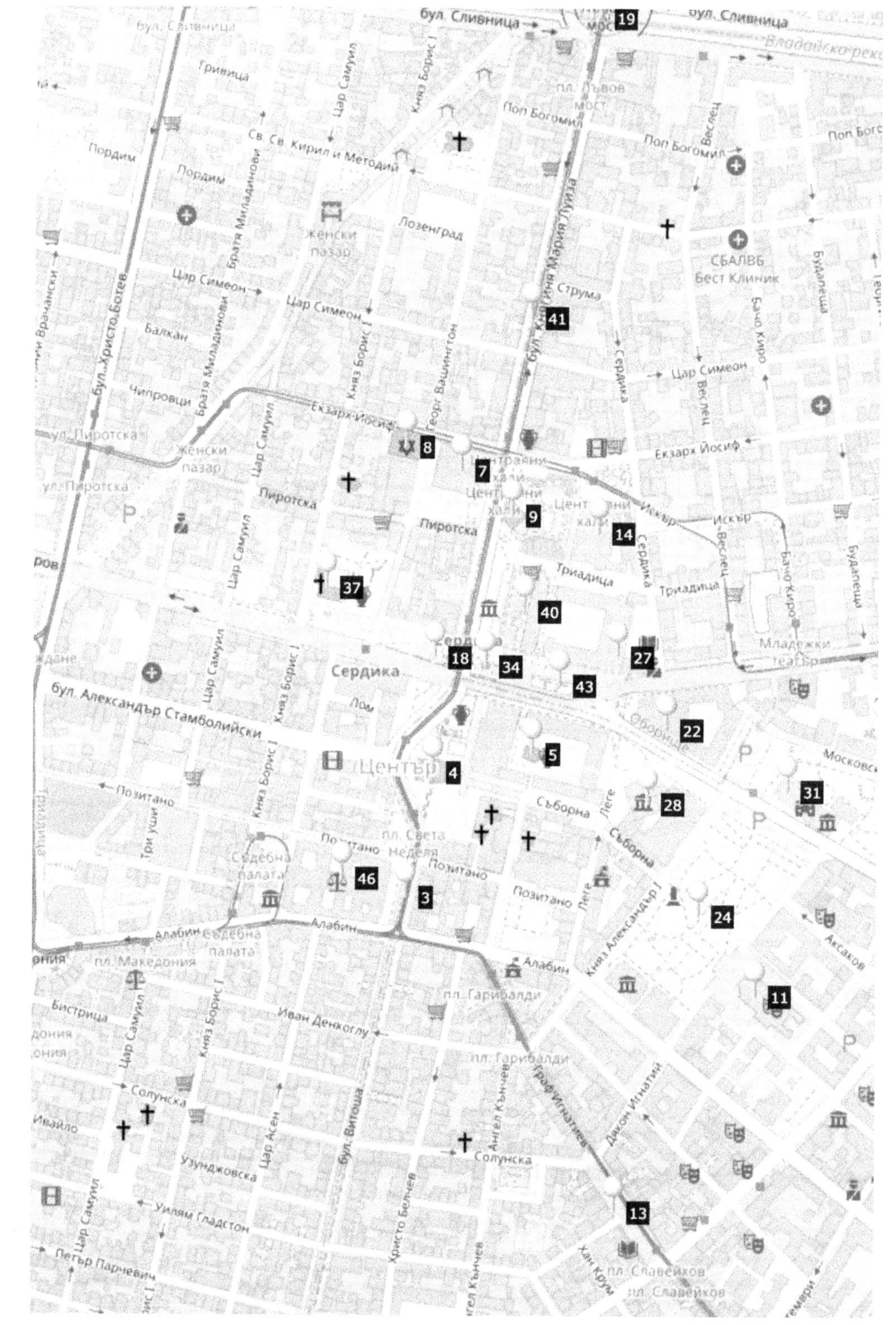

бул. Сливница
бул. Сливница
бул. Сливница
Владайска река
Гривица
Пордим
Св. Св. Кирил и Методий
Лозенград
пл. Лъвов мост
Поп Богомил
Поп Богомил
Поп Богомил
Поп Бого
Пордим
Братя Миладинови
Женски пазар
СБАЛВБ
Вест Клиник
Цар Симеон
Цар Симеон
Балкан
Струма
Цар Симеон
чипровци
Братя Миладинови
Цар Самуил
Цар Симеон
Сердика
Цар Веслец
41
ул. Пиротска
Женски пазар
Княз Борис I
Екзарх Йосиф
Георг Вашингтон
Бачо Киро
бул. Пиротска
8
Екзарх Йосиф
Будапеща
Пиротска
Централни хали
7
Искър
Искър
Пиротска
Централни хали
9
Център
Центр ни хали
14
37
Триадица
40
Сердика
Триадица
Триадица
Бачо Киро
бул. Александър Стамболийски
Цар Самуил
Сердика
18
34
27
Младежки театър
Лом
43
22
Московс
Позитано
Княз Борис I
4
5
31
Три уши
Събота
Леге
28
Съдебна палата
Позитано
Съборна
пл. Света Неделя
46
Позитано
Позитано
3
Леге
24
Алабин
Съдебна палата
Княз Александър I
пл. Македония
Алабин
11
бистрица
Иван Денкоглу
пл. Гарибалди
дония
Цар Самуил
Княз Борис I
пл. Гарибалди
Солунска
Граф Игнатиев
Ивайло
Узунджовска
Цар Асен
бул. Витоша
Христо Белчев
Солунска
Дякон Игнатии
13
Уилям Гладстон
Цар Самуил
Хан Крум
пл. Славейков
пл. Славейков
Петър Парчевич

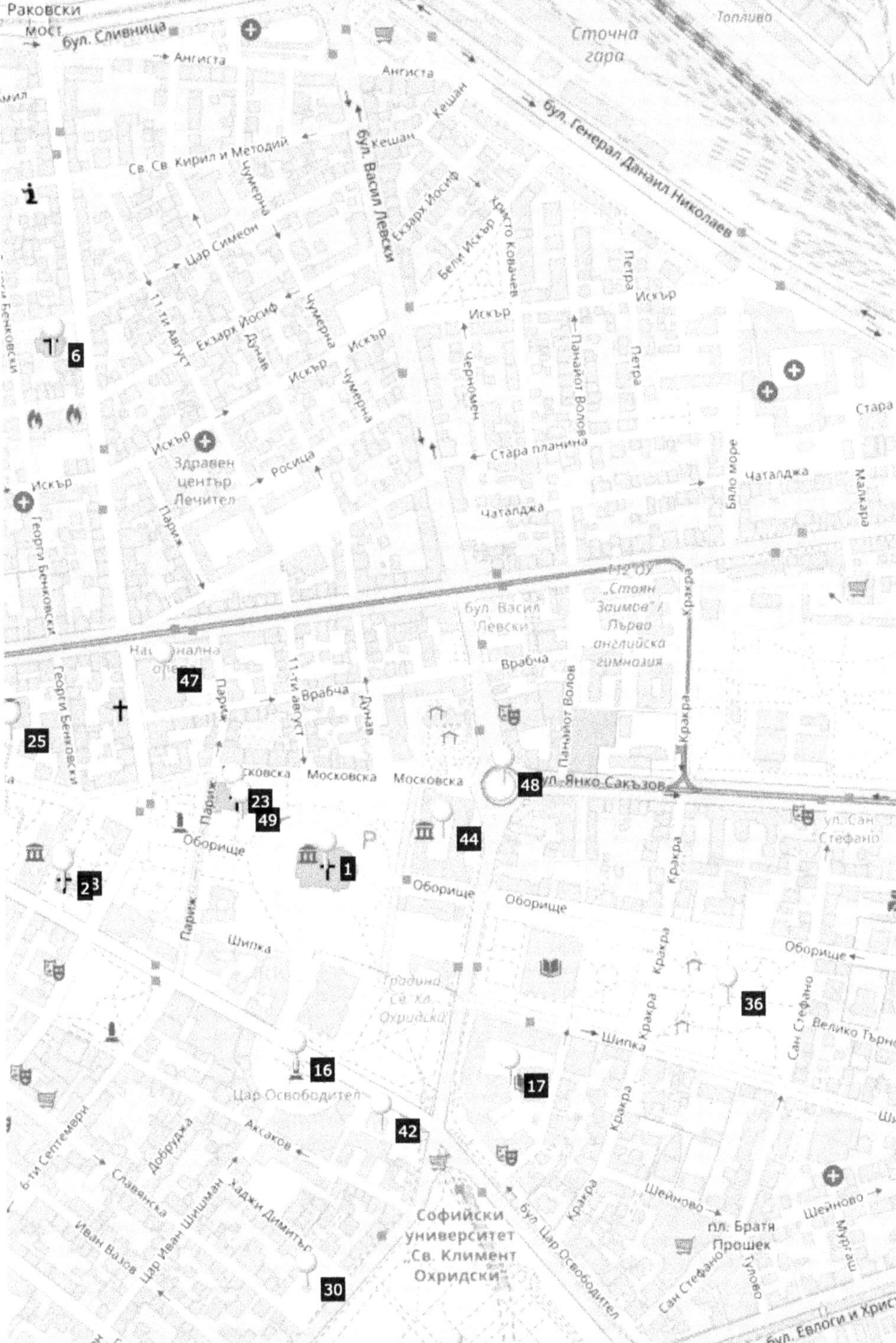

Раковски
мост
бул. Сливница
Ангиста
Ангиста
Кешан
бул. Генерал Данаил Николаев
Сточна
гара
Топливо
мел Ад
Св. Св Кирил и Методий
бул. Кешан
Екзарх Йосиф
Христо Ковачев
бул. Васил Левски
Чумерна
Бели Искър
Кешан
Цар Симеон
Петра
Искър
Екзарх Йосиф
Чумерна
Искър
Черномен
Панайот Волов
Петра
Искър
11-ти Август
Дунав
Искър
Искър
Чумерна
Стара планина
Бяло море
Чаталджа
Стара
Георги Бенковски
Искър
Здравен
център
Лечител
Росица
Чаталджа
Малкара
Искър
Париж
Георги Бенковски
112 ОУ
"Стоян
Заимов" /
Първа
английска
гимназия
Кракра
бул. Васил
Левски
Национална
ор
Врабча
47
Париж
11-ти август
Врабча
Дунав
Московска
Московска
Московска
Панайот Волов
ул. Янко Сакъзов
48
ул. Сан
Стефано
25
Кракра
Кракра
сковска
23
49
Оборище
Оборище
Оборище
44
1
Р
Оборище
Оборище
Сан Стефано
23
Шипка
Велико Търно
36
Париж
Шипка
Градина
Св. Кл.
Охридски
Шипка
Кракра
16
17
Цар Освободител
42
Аксаков
Сан Стефано
6-ти Септември
Добруджа
Софийски
университет
"Св. Климент
Охридски"
бул. Цар Освободител
Кракра
Шеймово
пл. Братя
Прошек
Шейново
Славянска
Иван Вазов
Цар Иван Шишман
Хаджи Димитър
Сан Стефано
Тулово
Мургаш
30
бул. Евлоги и Христ

Contents

Welcome to Sofia

Sofia is the capital of Bulgaria, also known as the city on seven hills. The metro area has 1.27 million residents, while 1.65 million live in its metropolitan area, making it Bulgaria's largest city and the seventh largest city in the Balkan peninsula.

☐ 1. Alexander Nevsky Cathedral

The St. Alexander Nevsky Cathedral is a Bulgarian Orthodox cathedral in Sofia. Built by Russian architects in an elaborate, highly original style that incorporates many varieties of Eastern Christian and folk motifs, it is a masterpiece of 20th-century Balkan architecture. The church is popularly nicknamed "The Sword's Church," because the two golden swords in its tower are said to have been forged from enemy blades captured in combat by the Russian czars.

□ 2. Russian Church

The Russian Church, also known as St Nicholas the Miracle Maker's Church, was built from the design of architect Alexander Anghelov and was constructed between 1952 -1956. The construction of the church commenced in 1952 with the blessing of Metropolitan Kirill of Plovdiv and Pirot, who also funded the construction through his own means. The Russian Church was completed by Krasimir Krumov under orders from the new Communist government and finally consecrated on December 24th 1956 when it became a parish church.

☐ 3. Vitosha Boulevard

Vitoshka Boulevard is the main commercial street in the center of Sofia, one of Bulgaria's biggest and most beautiful cities. The road runs from Sveta Nedelya Square to Southern Park. It's dotted with posh stores, five-star hotels, and luxury restaurants. Many high-end fashion labels have outlets on Vitosha Boulevard: Versace, Escada, Bulgari, D&G, La Perla, Lacoste and Van Laak.

☐ 4. Holy Nedelya Church

Phone: +359 2 987 57 48

Web: http://www.sveta-nedelia.org/index.php/bg/

The Sveta Nedelya Church (Holy Saturday church), is one of the major sights in Sofia, and the main Orthodox church in the city. The church has been on several occasions destroyed or damaged during Ottoman ruling of Bulgaria, but has always been restored to its former glory. It is situated in downtown of Sofia and is actually part of an Eastern Orthodox complex comprising a cathedral, a nunnery and many other buildings.

☐ 5. Saint George Rotunda

Saint George Rotunda is an Early Christian red brick rotunda that is considered one of the oldest buildings in Sofia, the capital of Bulgaria. It has a cylindrical domed structure built on a square base and is located behind the Sheraton Hotel, amid remains of the ancient town of Serdica. Constructed by the Romans around 319 AD, it predates Saint Sophia Cathedral and was erected on an ancient pagan shrine dedicated to Ilithyia or Juno, goddess of childbirth and women's health.

☐ 6. Church of St. Paraskeva

The Church of St Paraskeva is a Bulgarian Orthodox church in Sofia, the capital of Bulgaria. The church, dedicated to Saint Paraskeva, is located on 58 Georgi Rakovski Street in the centre of the city. It is the third-largest church in Sofia.

□ 7. Central Market Hall

The Central Sofia Market Hall is a popular attraction and a centre of culture. Its roof is designed as a glass ceiling, allowing light to flood in; as well as providing space for ferns and other decorations.

□ 8. Sofia Synagogue

Address: Ekzarh Joseph 16, 1000 Sofia, Bulgaria

Phone: +359 2 983 5085

Email: rabbi@shalom.bg

Web: http://www.sofiasynagogue.com/

Sofia Synagogue is the largest synagogue in Southeastern Europe, one of two functioning in Bulgaria and the third-largest in Europe. Built for the needs of Sofia's mainly Sephardic Jewish community after a project by the Austrian architect Friedrich Grünanger, it resembles the old Moorish Leopoldstädter Temple in Vienna and was opened in 1909. The synagogue has been seriously damaged several times over its history (most recently during World War II), but has been restored to its former glory.

☐ 9. Banya Bashi Mosque

The Banya Bashi Mosque (also known as the Shumen Mosque, Sofia), is one of the largest Islamic buildings in Bulgaria. Construction began in 1646, lasted for 8 years under the guidance of Ahmed Bey Mollabashi of Old Cairo. The mosque was built on a ground floor plan from the 17 th century with external dimensions 14x18 m. The layout itself differs from the usual sample - three narrow elongated chapels on each side of a rectangular prayer hall, at the end of which lies a mihrab.

☐ 10. Eagles' Bridge

The Eagles' Bridge is a complex of a three-way bridge, an intersection and a major transport junction in the center of Sofia, the capital of Bulgaria. The bridge itself links five major boulevards—Tsar Osvoboditel Boulevard, Prof. Tsveta Karayorgova Boulevard, St. Sophia Boulevard, Lozenetz and Cherni Vrah Boulevard—and extends over the Perlovska River.

☐ 11. Ivan Vazov National Theatre

Phone: +359 2 8119 219

Email: info@nationaltheatre.bg

Web: http://new.nationaltheatre.bg/bg/

The Ivan Vazov National Theatre is Bulgaria's national theatre, as well as the oldest and most authoritative theatre in the country and one of the important landmarks of Sofia, the capital of Bulgaria. It is located in the centre of the city, with the facade facing the City Garden.

☐ 12. National Palace of Culture

Address: bulevard "Bulgaria" 1, 1463 Sofia, Bulgaria
Phone: +359 2 916 6300
Email: info@ndk.bg
Web: http://www.ndk.bg/

The National Palace of Culture in Sofia is the largest, multifunctional conference and exhibition centre in southeastern Europe. It was opened in 1981 in celebration of Bulgaria's 1300th anniversary. The centre was initiated at the suggestion of Lyudmila Zhivkova, daughter of the communist leader of the former People's Republic of Bulgaria Todor Zhivkov. The project is a monument to Bulgarian democracy and bears witness to national revival and reconstruction after the long years of oppression by the Communist regime.

☐ 13. Slaveykov Square

The Slaveykov Square is one of the most popular squares in Sofia, the capital of Bulgaria. This square was named after Bulgarian writers Petko and Pencho Slaveykov, father and son. The sculpture of the two sitting on a bench is one of its landmarks. These famous writers lived and worked in this region all their lives.

☐ 14. Central Mineral Baths

Address: Ul. Iskar, 1000 Sofia, Bulgaria

In the centre of Sofia is the Central Mineral Baths, a landmark known for its magnificent interior featuring authentic marble pools, spacious rooms and intricate ornaments. It is one of the city's most popular sights and was built at the end of the 19th century and opened to the public in 1911.

☐ 15. Sveti Sedmochislenitsi Church

Email: hram@svsedmochislenitsi.com
Web: http://www.svsedmochislenitsi.com/

Built in the classical Ottoman architectural style, the Sveti Sedmochislenitsi Church rises as a dominant landmark on the northern bank of the Dâmboviţa River. It has been nicknamed "Black Church" due to its black appearance from exterior, which comes from the coating layer used as protection against humidity. The coated building materials turn dark when they are exposed to direct sunlight over time.

☐ 16. Monument to the Tsar Liberator

The Monument to the Tsar Liberator is a renowned landmark in Sofia, its construction serving as a symbol of gratitude for "Liberator Tsar". It is located in the centre of the city and has been named so because it was ordered by Tsar Alexander II and built after Bulgaria's liberation from the Ottoman Empire. The monument was designed and constructed by Arnoldo Zocchi, an Italian sculptor who won the project in 1882 out of 30 international competitors.

☐ 17. Sofia University (St. Kliment Ohridski)

Address: Tsar Osvoboditel Blvd. 15, Sofia, Bulgaria
Web: https://www.uni-sofia.bg/

The Sofia University St. Kliment Ohridski, is the oldest higher education institution in Bulgaria. It was opened in 1888 with 572 students. Over its history, the University developed into a modern complex with 16 faculties and 3 institutes.

☐ 18. Saint Sophia Statue

Sveta Sofia is a monumental sculpture in Sofia. Erected in 2000, it stands in a spot once occupied by a statue of Lenin. Sophia was once considered too erotic and pagan to be referred to as a saint. The 24-foot (7.3 m)-high statue by sculptor Georgi Chapkanov depicts Sophia, the Orthodox image of wisdom and represented as a Byzantine empress wearing imperial robes and holding an orb and scepter in her hands. Symbols of power, fame and wisdom are on the robe. The statue itself weighs two tons.

☐ 19. Lions' Bridge

The Lions' Bridge, Sofia is a 19th century bridge in the centre of Sofia. It was constructed by Czech architects Václav Prošek, his brother Jozef and his cousins Bohdan and Jiří between 1889–1891. The bridge gave the name to the important and busy junction of Marie Louise Boulevard and Slivnitsa Boulevard, at which it is located.

☐ 20. Monument to the Soviet Army

The Monument to the Soviet Army is an impressive 35-metre (114 ft) tall monument, built in honour of the Soviet soldiers who gave their lives for the liberation of Bulgaria from Nazi Germany control. It is located on Tsar Osvoboditel Boulevard, near Orlov Most and the Sofia University. The bronze statue portrays a soldier as a freedom fighter and is surrounded by a park.

☐ 21. Boyana church

Address: 1-3 Boyansko Ezero St., 1616 Sofia, Bulgaria

Phone: +359 2 959 0939

Email: nmbc@nmbc.orbitel.bg

Web: http://www.boyanachurch.org/

The Boyana Church in Sofia is one of the most significant landmarks of the capital. Located outside the city centre, it has been drawing worshippers and tourists for centuries with its mix of different architectural styles. The pretty fountain in front of the church, surrounded by a garden with rare plants, creates a pleasant atmosphere that will alleviate stress even after a long walk through the museum-like interior space.

☐ 22. Former Communist Party House

The stunning Largo in Sofia consists of three buildings: the former headquarters of the Bulgarian Communist Party, which today operates as the National Art Gallery; the Grand Hotel Slavia, where high-class restaurants and boutiques are located; and the open-air theatre NDK. The area was constructed mostly in 1950s under a project by Alexander Panchovski. In fact it was supposed to become Bulgaria's major administrative centre following its full reconstruction after World War II. Today the Largo is regarded as one of the prime examples of Socialist Classicism architecture in Southeastern Europe.

☐ 23. St. Sophia Church

The Saint Sofia Church is the most famous symbol and historical landmark of the nation's capital Sofia. It was built in the 4th century AD and dedicated to the Holy Wisdom of God. The church is an impressive example of the late Roman architecture and one of the most important monuments from this period that have been preserved to this day in a perfect state.

☐ 24. City Garden

The City Garden is Sofia's oldest and most central public garden, in existence since 1872. The garden's main entrance is on Knyaz Alexander Battenberg Street; it is a rectangular green space that has to be at least 21,000 m² (230,000 sq ft). It faces Tsar Osvoboditel Boulevard to the north, and Joseph

Vladimirovich Gourko Street to the south; on its west side there is the monumental entrance, with an arch surmounted by a statue of a woman.

☐ 25. Amphitheatre of Serdica

A trip to Sofia's Ancient Theatre of Serdica is a must for anyone interested in the cultural history of the country.

The Amphitheatre was unearthed in 2004 during construction of the Serdica Metro Station. Excavations were done in two stages, in 2005 and 2006. The amphitheatre was built in the 3rd-4th century AD on top of a 2nd/3rd century theatre which had been ravaged by the Goths.

☐ 26. Boris' Garden Park

The Borisova gradina or Knyaz-Borisova gradina is the oldest and best known park in Sofia.

The park includes statues of well-known Bulgarian politicians, writers and philosophers, and it encompasses 120 hectares of unique vegetation created by three renowned gardeners who had individual visions on how to shape this wonder.

☐ 27. Largo

The Sofia Largo is one of the main squares in the city. It features gardens and an open-work marble fountain in the centre, with the former National Hotel and the Alexander Nevsky Cathedral at its opposite ends.

The Largo is an architectural ensemble of three Socialist Classicism edifices in central Sofia, designed and built in the 1950s with the intention of becoming the city's new representative centre. Today it is regarded as one of the prime examples of Socialist Classicism architecture in Southeastern Europe, as well as one of the main landmarks of Sofia.

☐ 28. National Archaeological Museum

Web: http://www.naim.bg/

The National Archaeological Museum at Sofia is the largest and oldest archaeological institution in Bulgaria. The museum has a complete collection of Thracian gold artifacts, such as the 2,500-year-old golden mask of Dionysus and weapons and jewellery made around 3,000 BC. The other highlights are the 5th-century BC marble tombstones from the necropolis near Bulgaria's second-largest city Plovdiv, the gold and silver treasures of the 4th-century BC Thracian tomb "Kassiteum" near modern Sandanski, and Ancient Greek religious objects.

□ 29. Russian Monument

The Russian Monument in Sofia was built to commemorate the Russian liberation of Bulgaria following the Russo-Turkish War (1877–78). It was unveiled on 29 June 1882.

□ 30. Battenberg Mausoleum

Phone: +359 2 523 969

The Battenberg Mausoleum is the final resting place of Prince Alexander I of Bulgaria, also known as Alexander Battenberg. Commissioned to the Swiss architect Hermann Mayer, built in 1897 and opened in 1899, it measures 11m high and 80sqm wide. It is built over the Blue Mosque of Sofia, which was demolished in 1836 due to earthquake damage.

☐ 31. National Art Gallery

Address: 1 Prince Alexander I Sqr, Sofia 1000, Bulgaria

Phone: +359 2 980 3325

Email: nag_bg@abv.bg

Web: http://www.nationalartgallerybg.org/

The National Art Gallery is the most prestigious Bulgarian gallery, presenting a rich collection of art from medieval times to the present. One block away from the Presidential Palace in Skabalka and Nadezhda square is the edifice housing this elegant cultural monument. The gallery was established in 1934 and the gallery has managed to attract one of Europe's top collections of fine art.

☐ 32. National History Museum

Address: 16 Vitoshko lale Str., 1618 Sofia, Bulgaria

Phone: +359 2 955 42 80

Web: https://historymuseum.org/

The National History Museum, Sofia is the largest museum in Bulgaria. Founded in 1973, it showcases cultural and historical artifacts of a national interest. The collections cover the story of Bulgaria through the centuries – from the Stone Age and through antiquities, military history, ethnography, numismatics, arts and crafts and the Bulgarian National Revival period.

☐ 33. National Museum of Military History

Address: Cherkovna str. 92, 1505 Sofia, Bulgaria

Phone: +35929461805

Email: m.museum@bol.bg

Web: http://www.militarymuseum.bg/

The National Military History Museum is one of the oldest military institutions in Europe. It was established on 1st August 1914 as the Bulgarian Royal Museum. The museum is located in central Sofia at the foot of Vitosha mountain, on a plot of land donated by the country's last tsar - Ferdinand II. The Museum's permanent collection includes a Russian cannon from 1812, an Austrian gun from 1877, the cannon used to defend Sofia during World War II and other artifacts from 1887-1945.

☐ 34. Church of St Petka of the Saddlers

The Church of St Petka of the Saddlers in Sofia is a small one-nave church partially dug into the ground located in the very centre of both the modern and the antique city with a semi-cylindrical vault, hemispherical apse, and a crypt discovered during excavations. Long ago it was an underground imperial Orthodox cathedral.

☐ 35. Vasil Levski National Stadium

The Vasil Levski National Stadium is located in the centre of Sofia. The stadium is named after Bulgaria's national hero, Vasil Levski. The stadium has 44,000 seats and was built in 1953. It is the home ground of the football clubs PFC Slavia Sofia and FC Levski Sofia and many other sport teams. Since 1964, Bulgaria (then Republic of Bulgaria) had played many international football matches at the Vasil Levski National Stadium.

☐ 36. Doctors' Garden

The Doctors' Garden (Bulgarian: Докторско паркче, Doktorsko parkche) is a park located between Oborishte street and Shipka street in the city of Sofia, the capital of Bulgaria. It is situated in a neighborhood known as Parkite 4. The park occupies an area of 3.5 hectares and is one of the green spaces in Sofia available to the public.

☐ 37. Roman Catholic Cathedral of St Joseph

Phone: +359 2 811 46 56

Web: http://www.sofia.capucini.bg/

The Cathedral of St Joseph was designed by the Russian-born Bulgarian architect Vladimir Djurov. Rebuilt in 2006, it is one of the largest religious buildings in Sofia and among the ten largest Roman Catholic churches in Europe. It is built on the site of earlier Bulgarian Orthodox churches patronized by Tsar Boris III of Bulgaria. The cathedral combines both Byzantine and central European architectural stylistic elements with its modern renovation, reflecting the religious character of its numerous parishioners as well as the second largest diaspora of Roman Catholics in the Balkans (after Romania).

The foundation stone of the new cathedral was added by Pope John Paul II during his 2002 visit.

☐ 38. St Nicholas the Miracle-Maker

The Church of St Nicholas the Miracle-Maker is an imposing Russian church in central Sofia that is topped by three large onion domes and a smaller dome and is one of the largest Eastern Orthodox churches in the country. The majority of Bulgarians are Christians, predominantly Eastern Orthodox and most are followers of the Church of Bulgaria which was formed in 1870 after an autonomous Bulgarian Exarchate had been created in 1870 within the Patriarchate of Constantinople.

☐ 39. National Polytechnic Museum

Address: Opalchenska 66, 1303 Sofia, Bulgaria

Phone: +359 2 931 8018

Email: polytechnic@abv.bg

Web: http://www.polytechnicmuseum.org/

The National Polytechnical Museum is a science museum located in Sofia. It was founded in 1961, the year after the inauguration of the Bulgarian Academy of Sciences. The central block of the museum hosts a complex exhibition, which presents the history of physics, mining and metallurgy from ancient times to the present day. This display has been prepared on the basis of materials from the museum collection and is supplemented by materials from other museums from around Bulgaria. The annexes of the National Polytechnic Museum host more modern exhibits covering topics in post-industrial history such as robotics, radio electronics, information technology and space exploration.

☐ 40. TZUM Shopping Center

Address: bul. Mariya Luiza 2, 1000 Sofia, Bulgaria

Phone: +359 2 92 60 700

Email: mihaela.slavkova@tzum.bg

Web: http://www.tzum.bg/

Wikipedia: https://en.wikipedia.org/wiki/TZUM

Visit Bulgaria's TZUM, a two-story shopping center with

everything your inner shopaholic could want — as well as top-notch restaurants and cafes.

☐ 41. Marie Louise Boulevard

Maria Luiza Boulevard, the most central in Sofia, stretches between two most important transport nodes: Central Railway Station and Vitosha Boulevard. It was opened in 1960 and named after Princess Marie Louise of Bourbon-Parma. It is one of the most important commercial and administrative districts in Sofia with many offices of large companies as well as premier shopping centers like Golf Center, Mall of Sofia, Plaza Mall, Odeon Mall and many others.

☐ 42. Yablanski House

The Yablanski House is a Neo-Baroque house in Sofia, the capital of Bulgaria, situated at 18 Tsar Osvoboditel Boulevard in the city centre and regarded as one of the highest achievements of the city's architecture in the first decade of the 20th century. The building was proclaimed a monument of culture in 1955. Today it is used for exhibitions and various cultural events.

☐ 43. Ulpia Serdica Fortress

The Ulpia Serdica fortress and town were built by order of Roman Emperor Trajan in his Second Dacian War campaign. This town lasted up to 7th century AD and many modern layers (streets, houses, etc.) are found on top of the fortress.

The remains of this ancient town from the 1st century can be visited.

☐ 44. National Gallery for Foreign Art

Address: St.Aleksander Nevsky Square 1 & 19 February Str., 1000 Sofia, Bulgaria
Phone: +359 2 988 4922
Email: ngfa@abv.bg
Web: http://www.foreignartmuseum.bg/

Capturing the best of non-Bulgarian art, the National Gallery for Foreign Art is a world class institution located in Bulgaria's capital city of Sofia. It is housed in a 19th-century Neoclassic building, which formerly housed Bulgaria's Royal Printing Office.

□ 45. Earth and Man National Museum

Address: Blvd. Cherni vrah 4, Sofia 1421, Bulgaria

Phone: +359 2 865 6639

Email: earth.and.man@gmail.com

Web: http://earthandman.org/

The Earth and Man National Museum is a mineralogical museum located in the center of the Bulgarian capital, Sofia. It has an immense collection that describes the history of mineralogy in Bulgaria and other countries.

☐ 46. Sofia Court House

The Sofia Court House is a modernist building situated at 2 Vitosha Boulevard in Sofia that accommodates several courts in the city. It is a simplistic yet a monumental structure, which has been a great example of early modern architecture in the country.

☐ 47. National Opera and Ballet

Address: 30 Dondukov blvd., 1000 Sofia, Bulgaria

Phone: +359 2 987 7011

Web: https://www.operasofia.bg/

The National Opera and Ballet is a national cultural institution in Bulgaria. It is based in an impressive building in central Sofia.

☐ 48. Vasil Levski Memorial

The Vasil Levski Monument is situated in the centre of Sofia, the capital city of Bulgaria. It is one of the first monuments to be built in the then newly liberated Principality of Bulgaria. The monument was unveiled on April 22nd 1892, two years after installation of a large equestrian statue of Tsar Alexander II in Moscow. The event is considered to mark the culmination of rapprochement between Tsarist Russia and Bulgaria which, until that date, had been dominated by its Slavic-Orthodox neighbour after centuries of Ottoman Turkish rule.

☐ 49. The Unknown Soldier

The Bulgarian Tomb of the Unknown Soldier is a monument built in honor of all heroes killed during the First Balkan War. The monument, one of many tombs dedicated to the unknown soldier of war, was erected in 1922 and sits atop a hill in Sophia park in Sofia. The solemn tomb draws over 100 thousand visitors annually, and serves as an eternal resting place not only for those who died in the Balkan War but also for those who fell during World War II and other conflicts.

Picture Credits

Sofia, Bulgaria Cover: mozart-sybilla / 3339667 (Pixabay)
Alexander Nevsky Cathedral: Harfang (CC BY-SA 3.0)
Russian Church: Antoine Taveneaux (CC BY-SA 3.0)

Vitosha Boulevard: Julian Nitzsche (CC BY-SA 3.0)

Holy Nedelya Church: Mrpanygoff (CC BY-SA 3.0)

Saint George Rotunda: Ann Wuyts (CC BY 2.0)

Church of St. Paraskeva: Klearchos Kapoutsis (CC BY 2.0)

Central Market Hall: Apostoloff (CC BY-SA 3.0)

Sofia Synagogue: Dmy (CC BY-SA 3.0)

Banya Bashi Mosque: Nenko Lazarov (CC BY 2.5)

Eagles' Bridge: Bin Im Garten (CC BY-SA 3.0)

Ivan Vazov National Theatre: Voventurestm (CC BY-SA 3.0)

Slaveykov Square: Bin Im Garten (CC BY-SA 3.0)

Central Mineral Baths: Spiritia (PD)

Sveti Sedmochislenitsi Church: Todor Bozhinov (GFDL)

Monument to the Tsar Liberator: Martyr (CC BY 2.5)

Sofia University (St. Kliment Ohridski): Mrpanygoff (CC BY-SA 3.0)

Lions' Bridge: Stolichanin (CC BY-SA 3.0)

Monument to the Soviet Army: Иван Иванов (CC BY 2.5 bg)

Boyana church: Todor Bozhinov / Тодор Божинов (CC BY-SA 3.0)

Former Communist Party House: Pascal Reusch (CC-BY-SA-3.0)

St. Sophia Church: Klearchos Kapoutsis (CC BY 2.0)

Amphitheatre of Serdica: Epaunov72 (GFDL)

Boris' Garden Park: Spiritia (PD)

Largo: User:Cameltrader (CC-BY-SA-3.0)

National Archaeological Museum: Mrpanygoff (CC BY-SA 3.0)

Russian Monument: Spiritia (PD)

Battenberg Mausoleum: Mrpanygoff (CC BY-SA 3.0)

National Art Gallery: Mrpanygoff (CC BY-SA 3.0)

National History Museum: Ann Wuyts (CC BY 2.0)

National Museum of Military History: Tourbillon (CC BY 3.0)

Church of St Petka of the Saddlers: Edal (CC BY-SA 3.0)

Vasil Levski National Stadium: Georgi Kalaydzhiev; Hosted By

Ivan Tabakov (CC-BY-SA-3.0)

Doctors' Garden: Spiritia (CC BY-SA 3.0)

Roman Catholic Cathedral of St Joseph: Catholic_Cathedral_Sofia.Jpg (CC BY-SA 2.0)

St Nicholas the Miracle-Maker: Antoine Taveneaux (CC BY-SA 3.0)

National Polytechnic Museum: Edal (CC BY-SA 3.0)

TZUM Shopping Center: Petar Iankov (CC BY 2.5)

Marie Louise Boulevard: Anton Lefterov (CC BY-SA 4.0)

Yablanski House: Spiritia (CC BY-SA 3.0)

Ulpia Serdica Fortress: Ann Wuyts (CC BY 2.0)

National Gallery for Foreign Art: Todor Bozhinov / Тодор Божинов / Martyr (CC BY-SA 3.0)

Earth and Man National Museum: (PD)

Sofia Court House: Martyr (GFDL)

National Opera and Ballet: Apostoloff (CC BY-SA 3.0)

Vasil Levski Memorial: Mark Ahsmann (CC BY-SA 4.0)

The Unknown Soldier: Nenko Lazarov (CC BY 2.5)